W9-BRT-272

COLORADO
ROCKIES

by Brian Howell

Published by ABDO Publishing Company, 8000 West 78th Street, Edina, Minnesota 55439. Copyright © 2011 by Abdo Consulting Group, Inc. International copyrights reserved in all countries. No part of this book may be reproduced in any form without written permission from the publisher. SportsZone™ is a trademark and logo of ABDO Publishing Company.

Printed in the United States of America,
North Mankato, Minnesota
112010
012011

Editor: Matt Tustison
Copy Editor: Nicholas Cafarelli
Interior Design and Production: Carol Castro
Cover Design: Christa Schneider

Photo Credits: Nick Wass/AP Images, cover; David Zalubowski/AP Images, title, 4, 9, 12, 40, 42 (top), 43 (top and bottom), 47; Jack Dempsey/AP Images, 7, 30, 34, 42 (bottom), 43 (middle); Eric Gay/AP Images, 11; Carlos Osorio/AP Images, 15; Ron Frehm/AP Images, 16; Mark Reis/AP Images, 18, 42 (middle); Photo by Rogers Photo Archive/Getty Images, 21; Getty Images, 23; Otto Greule Jr. /Allsport via Getty Images, 25; Joe Mahoney/AP Images, 26; Ed Andrieski/ AP Images, 29, 33; Lenny Ignelzi/AP Images, 37; Gene J. Puskar, File/AP Images, 39; Susan Sterner/AP Images, 44

Library of Congress Cataloging-in-Publication Data
Howell, Brian, 1974-
  Colorado Rockies / by Brian Howell.
      p. cm. — (Inside MLB)
  Includes index.
  ISBN 978-1-61714-042-6
  1. Colorado Rockies (Baseball team)—History—Juvenile literature. I. Title.
  GV875.C78H69 2011
  796.357'640978883—dc22
                        2010036561

TABLE OF CONTENTS

CHAPTER 1

ROCKTOBER

Many fans of the San Diego Padres would argue that the greatest moment in Colorado Rockies history really should not count. Those Padres fans might be right.

When the 2007 regular season came to a close, the Padres and the Rockies were tied with 89–73 records. One of them would be going to the National League (NL) playoffs as a wild-card team. The other would be going home for the winter. To determine which team would make the postseason, they played a one-game playoff on October 1 in Denver, Colorado.

That night, in the bottom of the 13th inning, the Rockies' Jamey Carroll hit a fly ball to right field. After San Diego's Brian Giles caught the ball, Colorado's Matt Holliday sprinted toward the plate and slid head first. He was ruled

Todd Helton watches his home run during the Rockies' 9–8, 13-inning win over the Padres in a one-game NL West playoff on October 1, 2007.

safe by the home-plate umpire. The fans at Coors Field went crazy. The Rockies went crazy. For the first time in 12 seasons, Colorado was headed to the playoffs.

"Rocktober," as it came to be known—combining Rockies and October—was born. The Rockies would carry that momentum all the way to the World Series.

In the days after that game, Padres fans—and some players—argued that Holliday never did touch home plate on his slide. Even videos of the play make it difficult to tell for sure whether he touched the plate. Not that it mattered to the Rockies. Holliday was ruled safe. Nobody could ever take that away from him or Colorado. It was a close play. But it worked out.

"Yeah, I was going to go for it," Holliday said of the final play. "You've got to figure you just play the game at that point and let your instincts take over."

Holliday's awkward slide left him with a bloody chin and some bruises. But that moment became the one most fans remember from the thrilling 2007 season.

Before 2007, the Rockies had six consecutive losing seasons. For a while, the 2007 campaign had the look of another disappointing season. Late in the year, the Rockies had improved. But they still did not look like a playoff team. They were 6 1/2 games out of first place in the NL West Division with 13 games to play. What happened from there will forever be remembered in Colorado sports history. Including their epic victory over the Padres in that one-game playoff, the Rockies won 14 of their final

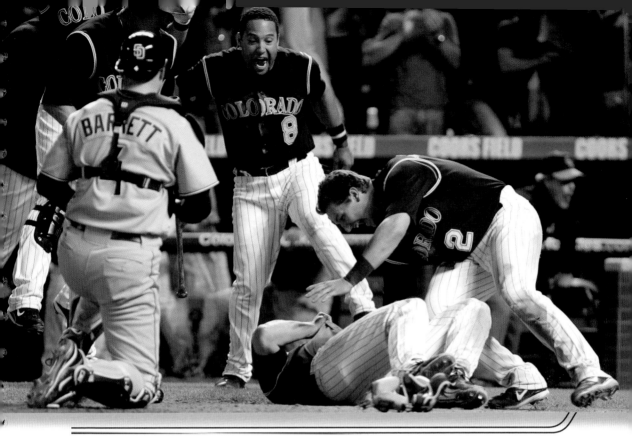

A banged-up Matt Holliday lies on the ground after scoring the winning run as Colorado teammates celebrate a 9–8 victory over San Diego for the 2007 NL West crown.

15 games of the regular season to get into the postseason.

"We never give up. We always battle," catcher Yorvit Torrealba said after the Rockies beat the Padres in the one-game playoff.

Colorado proved Torrealba's words several times during its season-ending hot streak.

Todd Helton hit a game-winning, two-run home run in the ninth inning against the visiting Los Angeles Dodgers one night. Three nights later, Brad Hawpe connected for a 14th-inning homer that proved to be the game-winner in a victory over the host Padres. Hawpe had a two-run double in

WORTH THE WAIT

Through Todd Helton's first 10 major league seasons, all with Colorado, the Rockies never finished higher than third in the NL West Division. He was an All-Star five times during that period. In 2000, he led the NL with a .372 batting average and 147 runs batted in (RBIs) and also hit 42 home runs.

Before his 11th season, in 2007, the Rockies nearly traded Helton to the Boston Red Sox. The deal never happened, however. The first baseman stayed with Colorado. Then, in 2007, the Rockies—with Helton—finally got to the postseason. It took him 1,578 regular-season games to get there.

"I don't know how to explain it," Helton said after the Rockies earned a playoff berth. "To put this into words, you can't do it. I'm so happy to do it here in Colorado and be a part of this right now. It's crazy. Look at this [celebration]. This is what it's all about right here."

Colorado's 4–3 win over visiting Arizona on the last day of the regular season. The win forced the one-game playoff against San Diego.

"We believe that we're good enough to be where we are," pitcher Jeff Francis said after the Rockies beat the Padres and qualified for the postseason.

As it turned out, the thrilling victory over the Padres was just the beginning. In the first round of the playoffs, the Rockies swept the Philadelphia Phillies three games to none in the NL Division Series (NLDS). Then, in the NL Championship Series (NLCS), Colorado swept Arizona four

First baseman Todd Helton, *left*, and shortstop Troy Tulowitzki are ecstatic after the Rockies swept the Diamondbacks in the 2007 NLCS.

games to none. The Rockies went into the World Series with a 21–1 record over their previous 22 games.

"Everything just came together for us," Holliday said. "It'll be hard for anybody to duplicate that."

Unfortunately for the Rockies, the magic ended there. They never won a game in the World Series. They were dominated by the American League (AL) champion Boston Red Sox. Boston won four games to none. The Series defeat did not diminish Colorado's 2007 season, however. Maybe Holliday did not touch the plate. Maybe what might have been the greatest moment in Rockies history should not have counted. But it did count and the Rockies will never

forget it. Holliday's slide. The 21–1 streak. The end-of-season drama. The 2007 season was one out of a storybook. No matter what else the Rockies do in their history, 2007 will never be forgotten.

Star Performances

In 2007, left fielder Matt Holliday, shortstop Troy Tulowitzki, and pitcher Jeff Francis had some of the best seasons in Rockies history. Holliday won the NL batting title with a .340 average and hit 36 home runs with 137 RBIs. He was second in the NL Most Valuable Player (MVP) Award voting. Tulowitzki finished second in the NL Rookie of the Year voting. He hit .291 with 24 homers and 99 RBIs. Francis went 17–9 with a 4.22 earned-run average (ERA). The left-hander tied the team mark for wins and was ninth in the NL Cy Young Award voting. Manager Clint Hurdle, meanwhile, finished third in the NL Manager of the Year voting.

Colorado's Troy Tulowitzki, *top*, holds his head down as Boston players celebrate winning the World Series on October 28, 2007, in Denver.

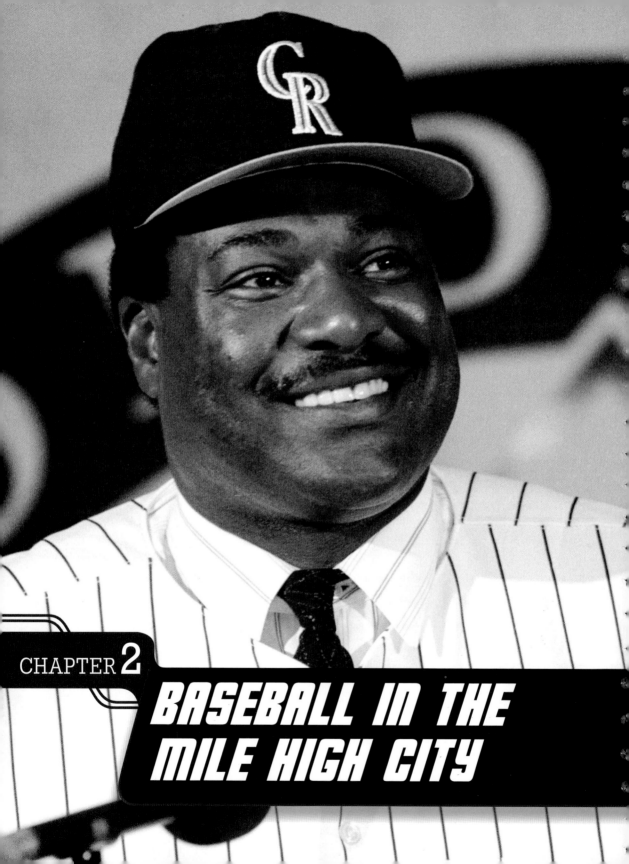

CHAPTER 2

BASEBALL IN THE MILE HIGH CITY

Denver's professional baseball history goes back to the 1800s. And, for much of the 1900s, a pro team was located in town. The Denver Grizzlies, who later became known as the Bears, were regular members of the Western League from 1901 through the mid-1950s. The Western League was a minor league. In 1955, the Bears joined the American Association, a Triple-A minor league.

The Denver Bears, who were renamed the Zephyrs in 1984, were a minor league team for several major league teams. The Mile High City supported its team. But fans thirsted for big-league baseball.

Denver's dream finally came true on July 5, 1991. On that day, the owners of the 26 teams in Major League Baseball (MLB) voted unanimously to add NL teams in Denver and Miami. The Denver team was

Former big-league slugger Don Baylor smiles on October 28, 1992, after he was named the first manager of the Rockies.

DON BAYLOR

As the first manager of the Rockies, Don Baylor left no doubt he was running the team on the field. "He was tough but fair," pitcher Curtis Leskanic said.

From 1970 to 1988, Baylor played for six major league teams. He won the AL MVP Award in 1979 with the California Angels. That season, the outfielder/designated hitter batted .296 with 36 home runs. He led the league in runs scored (120) and RBIs (139) and helped the Angels win the AL West title. He went on to become a member of the 1987 Minnesota Twins team that won the World Series. Baylor was a power hitter known for crowding the plate. As a result, he was often hit by pitches. He was hit by a pitch 267 times in his career. That was the fourth-highest total in big-league history through 2010.

Baylor managed the Rockies for six years, from 1993 to 1998. He led them to three winning seasons.

named the Colorado Rockies to represent the entire state. The Miami team would be known as the Florida Marlins. The name Rockies came from the majestic Rocky Mountains, which sit to the west of Denver.

After the 1991 announcement, the Rockies still had nearly two years until they would actually begin playing. So, the organization focused on building a team. The Rockies hired staff members, fielded a minor league team beginning in the spring of 1992, and then began filling the major league roster in the fall of 1992. Don Baylor, a former big-league player who was the 1979 AL MVP, was hired as the Rockies' first manager.

The first player of note in Rockies history was Andres Galarraga. He signed with the team on November 16,

The Rockies' Andres Galarraga, *left*, poses with the Blue Jays' John Olerud at the 1993 All-Star Game in Baltimore. Both players won batting titles that season.

1992. At the time, Galarraga was an eight-year veteran and a former All-Star. But his production had declined. If it were not for Baylor being in Denver, Galarraga might not have ever come to town. Baylor was Galarraga's hitting coach with the St. Louis Cardinals in 1992.

"The Big Cat"

Andres "The Big Cat" Galarraga played five seasons in Colorado and was the Rockies' first true star. He won the NL batting title in 1993 with a .370 average. In those five seasons, he averaged 34 home runs and 116 RBIs per season. Galarraga got his nickname, though, because of his defense. The big first baseman was quick on his feet.

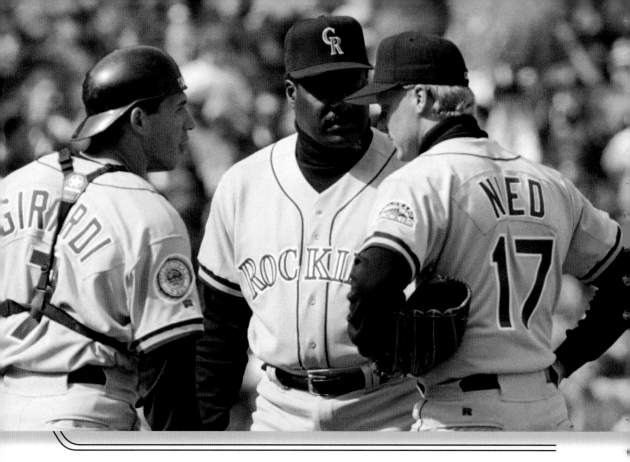

Manager Don Baylor, *middle*, meets with catcher Joe Girardi, *left*, and pitcher David Nied during the Rockies' first regular-season game ever. It was on April 5, 1993, against the host Mets. Colorado lost 3–0.

He saw enough in Galarraga to believe he could return to glory. Boy, was he right. Galarraga went on to win the NL batting title in 1993.

The day after Galarraga signed, the Rockies and the Marlins participated in an expansion draft. The teams selected players from other major league squads. Through that draft process, the Rockies picked up many of their first stars. Among them were third basemen Charlie Hayes and Vinny Castilla, second baseman Eric Young, and pitcher Armando Reynoso.

Finally, Colorado fans had real major league players for whom they could root. The fans turned out in droves to watch the team play in its first season, in 1993. That season, and in 1994, the Rockies played at Mile High Stadium. That stadium was the home of the NFL's Denver Broncos and the former home of the minor league Zephyrs baseball team. The stadium held more than 80,000 fans—much more than the other baseball parks in the major leagues.

It was not too surprising that the Rockies shattered attendance records. They drew 80,227 fans for the team's first home game ever. It was an 11–4 win over the Montreal Expos on April 9, 1993. This broke the major leagues' single-game attendance record. The Rockies also set the big-league single-season attendance record with

Welcome to Denver

On April 9, 1993, the long wait for Denver fans ended when the Rockies played their first home game. Colorado opened the 1993 season with two losses on the road to the New York Mets. Then, the Rockies returned to Denver to face the Montreal Expos on April 9. Colorado beat Montreal 11–4 at Mile High Stadium. The Rockies' Eric Young hit two homers, including a leadoff shot. "I played 18 years in the big leagues, and I don't ever remember people being as excited during a game as that one," said outfielder Dale Murphy, who played his final season in 1993 with Colorado.

4,483,350 fans in 1993. In 1994, the team had even more fans per game come through Mile High Stadium's gates.

The Rockies did not win much those first two years. They went a combined 120–159. But the fans did not care. Finally, big-league baseball was in Denver.

CHAPTER **3**

A GRAND NEW
BALLPARK

Before Colorado was given a big-league team in 1991, a deal was in place to build a new baseball stadium. During the Rockies' first two seasons, in 1993 and 1994, they shared Mile High Stadium with the Denver Broncos football team while the Rockies' new stadium was being built.

Construction on the new stadium began in the fall of 1992. The Rockies moved into brand-new Coors Field in 1995. Many baseball followers considered it one of the sport's finest stadiums. It was designed to highlight one of Colorado's greatest features, the Rocky Mountains. On a clear day, fans can see the mountains from their seats. Beyond center field, there is a mountain setting, with pine trees, rocks, and a waterfall. The park also replicates some of the features that made old ballparks unique, such as the manually

The Rockies' new home ballpark, Coors Field, is shown in March 1995 with the Denver skyline in the background.

operated scoreboard in right field. At first, the stadium was planned to hold about 43,000 fans. Because of the popularity of the team in 1993 and 1994, however, plans changed so it could seat more than 50,000.

When Coors Field opened in 1995, it got off to a great start. The first game was played there on April 26, 1995, against the New York Mets. It ended when Dante Bichette hit a game-winning three-run home run in the bottom of the 14th inning. That was an unforgettable start to an unforgettable year for the Rockies, and for Bichette.

"Of all the teams I played on, that was probably the one that I had the most fun on," shortstop Walt Weiss said. "We were just very close as a team. We had real good chemistry. We had a real good lineup and had this new ballpark that we really took advantage of. Teams would come in [to Coors Field] and not know what to make of it, and we used that to our advantage."

The 1995 season started late and was shortened to 144 games. This was because an MLB strike from the previous season was not settled until

Dante Bichette swings in 1995. Playing his home games in the hitter-friendly Coors Field, Bichette batted .340 and smashed 40 homers.

ROCKIES' MVP

Some Rockies fans still believe that outfielder Dante Bichette should have been named the NL MVP in 1995. Bichette led the league in home runs (40) and RBIs (128) while batting .340. But he wound up finishing second to Cincinnati Reds shortstop Barry Larkin in the MVP voting. It was one of many standout seasons with the Rockies for Bichette. In seven years with the team, he was a four-time All-Star and hit 201 home runs.

Bichette broke into the big leagues in 1988 with the California Angels and played with them through 1990. He then was traded to the Milwaukee Brewers and was with them in 1991 and 1992. Milwaukee then dealt him to Colorado before the Rockies' first-ever season in 1993.

Bichette found a home in Colorado. In his seven seasons with the Rockies, Bichette hit more than 20 homers seven times, batted better than .300 six times, and surpassed 100 RBIs five times.

just before the 1995 season was originally scheduled to begin. The Rockies started 7–1 in 1995 and played well all season. Colorado finished 77–67, one game behind the Los Angeles Dodgers in the NL West Division standings. The Rockies defeated the visiting San Francisco Giants 10–9 on the last day of the season to get into the playoffs as the NL wild-card team. In only their third season, the Rockies were headed to the postseason.

"Having an entire stadium full of people jumping up and down and having every one of your teammates hugging you . . . obviously, that's a memory I'll always cherish," said pitcher Curtis Leskanic, who recorded the final outs in that win over the Giants.

In the 1995 playoffs, the Rockies were the NL wild-card team. In 1994, MLB

Vinny Castilla congratulates Larry Walker, *right*, and Dante Bichette, *middle*, after they scored on Walker's three-run homer in Game 2 of the 1995 NLDS. Colorado lost the game 7–4 and the series in four games.

reorganized the NL and the AL into leagues with three divisions each. Previously, the leagues had two divisions each. The new playoff system would not go into effect until 1995 because the 1994 strike prevented a postseason from occurring. Beginning in 1995, the three division winners from each league plus the team from each league that had the best record without winning its division would make the playoffs.

The 1995 Rockies lost three games to one to the NL East-champion Atlanta Braves in the best-of-five NLDS. Colorado had the lead in all four games but could only hang on to beat Atlanta one time. The NLDS defeat could not take away from the great season the Rockies had, however. "It was just a great time, for the team, for the city, for everybody associated with the Colorado Rockies," Bichette said.

During the 1995 season, the Rockies were one of the most powerful teams in baseball. Bichette hit .340 and led the NL in home runs (40) and

Fantastic Finishers

The Rockies have not always had the best of luck with pitchers. But one of the main reasons they reached the playoffs in 1995 was their bullpen. Led by Darren Holmes, Curtis Leskanic, and Steve Reed, Colorado had one of the top groups of relief pitchers in the NL. During their careers, those three pitched in a combined 1,080 games for the Rockies. They are still regarded as three of the best relief pitchers in team history.

RBIs (128). In fact, four of the top eight home-run hitters in the NL played for the Rockies—Bichette (40 homers), Larry Walker (36), Vinny Castilla (32), and Andres Galarraga (31). The Rockies became just the second team—and the first since the 1977 Los Angeles Dodgers—in baseball history to have four players with 30 or more home runs. But that season was just the beginning for Colorado. The Rockies also had four 30-home run hitters in 1996, 1997, and 1999.

Reaching the playoffs made for a grand first year at Coors Field. It was a year filled with a lot of wins and a lot of home runs. The wins would not come as easily in future years. But the home runs would. In 1996, there were more home runs hit at Coors Field (271 between the Rockies and their opponents) than in any other ballpark in

Colorado's Vinny Castilla follows through on a swing in 1995. Castilla hit 32 home runs that season, and the Rockies had an NL-best 200.

major league history. In 1999, that record was broken, with 303 homers hit at Coors Field. The stadium's reputation for being a hitter's paradise began in 1995 and continued for years.

As for the Rockies, the 1995 season was a special one that ended with the team's first playoff appearance. In 1996, Colorado picked up more victories (83) than the team ever had before. The Rockies then matched that win total in 1997. Both seasons ended with third-place finishes, however. After 1995, in fact, Colorado would not get back to the playoffs until 2007.

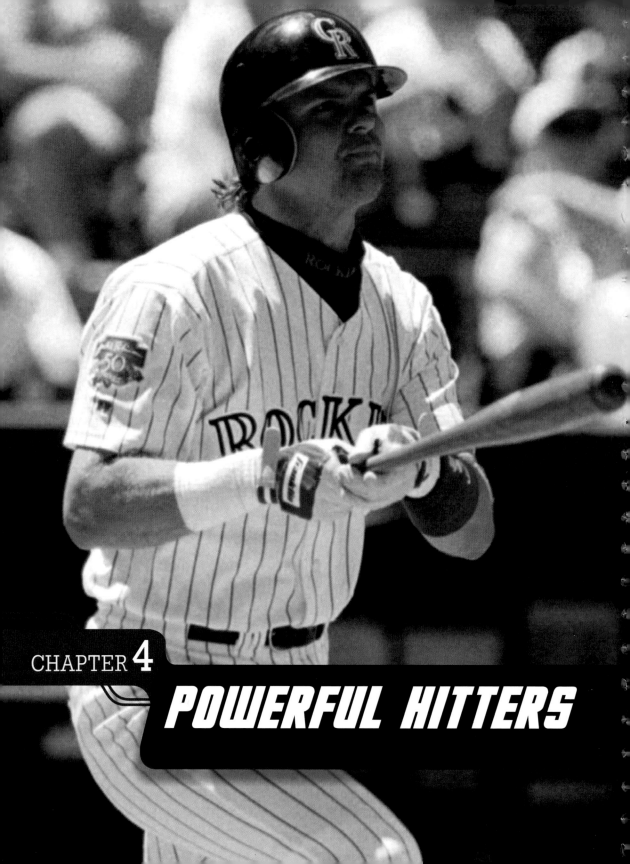

CHAPTER 4

POWERFUL HITTERS

Throughout much of the Rockies' history, they have been known for two things: power hitters and struggling pitchers. They have, of course, had pitchers who have done well, especially in recent years. For the most part, however, Colorado has struggled to find pitchers who could succeed in Coors Field.

As far back as 1993, the Rockies' first season, they have had great offensive players. That season, Dante Bichette and Charlie Hayes had the best statistical seasons of their careers. Andres Galarraga won the NL batting title in 1993 with a .370 average and went on to have five standout years with the Rockies.

Coors Field quickly gained a reputation for being a hitter's park. Fly balls that often would be outs in other parks turned into home runs at Coors Field.

The Rockies' Larry Walker watches a ball he hit in 1997. Walker batted .366 with 49 homers and 130 RBIs that year and was chosen NL MVP.

Hitters loved it there. But pitchers hated it because runs piled on the scoreboard like at no other stadium.

By 1995, Bichette and Galarraga had established themselves as fan favorites and two of the most powerful hitters in the NL. But the duo was not alone.

Vinny Castilla was an original Rockie who played mostly in a backup role in 1993 and 1994. When Hayes left the team after the 1994 season, Castilla replaced him as the starting third baseman. Castilla's career took off from there. In 1995, he hit 32 home runs. That season started a remarkable five-year stretch for Castilla with the Rockies. From 1995 to 1999, he hit at least 40 homers three times and drove in at least 102 runs four times. Castilla's best season was in 1998, when he hit .319 with 46 homers and 144 RBIs. He was traded after the 1999 season but returned to the Rockies in 2004 and hit 35 homers and drove in 131 runs. Castilla retired in 2006 as one of the most popular players in team history, especially with Denver's large Hispanic-American population. "We developed a good relationship, me and the people of Colorado," he said.

Joining the team in 1995 was right fielder Larry Walker.

Altitude Adjustment

What made Coors Field so tough on pitchers? Denver's high altitude—5,280 feet (1,609 m) above sea level—created dry air that took the moisture out of the baseballs. That caused the ball to fly through the air farther and faster than at lower elevations. Because of that, home runs came in bunches at Coors Field. "I hit some balls in [batting practice] that I thought were pop-ups, and they went out—to the opposite field. Wow," New York Yankees shortstop Derek Jeter said after the 1998 All-Star Game at Coors Field.

Third baseman Vinny Castilla makes a throw on the run in 1998. Castilla, a fan favorite with Colorado, enjoyed a career-best year that season.

Walker had already been an All-Star and a Gold Glove Award winner with the Montreal Expos. Walker quickly proved he belonged in the powerful Rockies lineup. Some believe to this day that he was the best player to ever suit up for Colorado. Walker won three NL batting titles from 1998 to 2001. He was named the NL MVP in 1997. He became the first Rockies player to earn that award. During his 10 seasons with Colorado, he was considered by many baseball followers as one of the best players in the sport, on offense and defense.

Todd Helton was another Rockies star. Drafted by

Colorado, he took over the starting job at first base when Galarraga left after the 1997 season. As good as Galarraga was in a Rockies uniform, Helton had even more impressive statistics. If Walker is not the best Rockie ever, the honor might go to Helton. He was the NL batting champion in 2000, an All-Star each season from 2000 to 2004, and a Gold Glove Award winner in 2001, 2002, and 2004. As of the 2010 season, Helton was still a Rockie. He had more runs scored, hits, doubles, home runs, RBIs, walks, and games played than any other player in team history.

Bichette, Castilla, Galarraga, Helton, and Walker were the biggest offensive stars to play for the Rockies. But they

Todd Helton

When Todd Helton was awarded Colorado's starting job at first base as a rookie in 1998, he had a tough task in replacing the popular Andres Galarraga. Helton did not take long to prove he was a worthy successor. Helton developed into a player whom some baseball followers regard as the best in Rockies history. "To do what he's done in the game, I mean, it's pretty phenomenal," former Colorado outfielder Matt Holliday said. Each season from 1998 through 2004, Helton batted at least .315, hit at least 25 homers, and had at least 96 RBIs. His finest season was in 2000, when he led the NL in batting average (.372), RBIs (147), hits (216), and doubles (59).

were not the only ones. Ellis Burks, Jeromy Burnitz, Jeff Cirillo, Jeffrey Hammonds, Jay Payton, and Preston Wilson were among the other hitters who had some of the best years of their careers after arriving in Colorado.

Todd Helton completes a swing in 2000. The first baseman emerged as yet another slugger for the Rockies' powerful offense.

LARRY WALKER

Few players in Rockies history were as talented as right fielder Larry Walker. He was one of the NL's best overall hitters. He played exceptional defense and had a strong arm. He was also a smart base runner. Not bad for a guy who grew up in Canada and hoped to be a hockey star.

"I played with some great players, but he's right there at the top of the list," former Rockies shortstop Walt Weiss said.

Walker broke into the major leagues in 1989 with the Montreal Expos. Before the 1995 season, he signed with the Rockies. In 1997, he batted .366 with 49 homers, 130 RBIs, and 33 stolen bases and was named the NL's MVP. Walker went on to win three batting titles (.363 in 1998, .379 in 1999, and .350 in 2001) with Colorado. The Rockies traded Walker to the St. Louis Cardinals during the 2004 season. He played for St. Louis through 2005, then retired.

With so much firepower on offense, the Rockies figured all they needed to be a great team was good pitching. They tried to get it too. Colorado traded for former Cy Young Award winner Bret Saberhagen in 1995. The team signed free agent Darryl Kile in 1998. Then, in 2001, the Rockies signed All-Stars Mike Hampton and Denny Neagle to contracts worth more than $225 million. None of the moves worked. Saberhagen, Kile, Hampton, and Neagle all struggled as Rockies, in large part because of the ballpark.

"Pitching in Coors can be mentally draining," said Jason Jennings, who was one of the few pitchers who had success in Colorado. "You have to concentrate harder than normal, and you have to fight the frustration when your ball doesn't break or sink as much as it

Mike Hampton pitches in 2001. Hampton, like many other Rockies pitchers, struggled to succeed in Colorado's mile-high altitude.

does [in other ballparks]. But if you back off and try to be too careful, it just gets worse."

The combination of great hitting and poor pitching was a bad mix for the Rockies. In the nine seasons from 1998 to 2006, the Rockies finished no better than fourth in the NL West Division. Only once in those nine years did they have a winning record, at 82–80 in 2000. Entering the 2007 season, the Rockies were a struggling team still looking to regain the magic they had discovered in 1995.

CHAPTER 5

BUILDING A WINNER

The 2006 season was another disappointment for the Rockies. But they had hope that 2007 would be better. The offense, as usual, had plenty of great hitters. They included youngsters Garrett Atkins, Brad Hawpe, and Matt Holliday. Todd Helton was still among the top hitters in the NL as well. Colorado also had speedsters Willy Taveras and Kazuo Matsui at the top of the batting order.

"One of these years, we're going to make a huge step," general manager Dan O'Dowd said at spring training in 2007. "Maybe this is the year."

The fans and media were not as optimistic. After the Rockies lost 6–5 to the host Arizona Diamondbacks on May 21, they dropped to 18–27. The 2007 season looked like another disappointment. From that point on, however, the Rockies played better than they ever

Troy Tulowitzki rounds the bases after hitting a home run in 2007. Despite being a rookie, the shortstop became a leader for Colorado.

had before. Colorado reached the playoffs that season and defeated the Philadelphia Phillies and Arizona to reach the World Series for the first time.

Colorado discovered a new star in 2007. Rookie Troy Tulowitzki entered spring training that year competing with Clint Barmes for the starting shortstop job. Tulowitzki, a first-round draft pick in 2005, won the job. After a slow start, he became one of the team's most important players. That season, he was one of the top all-around shortstops in baseball. He played excellent defense and swung a powerful bat. He finished second in the NL Rookie of the Year voting. He finished just behind the Milwaukee Brewers' Ryan Braun. More than anything, Tulowitzki brought a hunger to win and proved to be a leader, despite his youth.

Another key to Colorado's success in 2007 was its pitching. After years of struggling on the mound, the Rockies seemed to figure it out that season. Jeff Francis tied a team record with 17 wins. Aaron Cook was stellar when he was healthy. Josh Fogg earned the nickname "The Dragonslayer." This was because of his ability to pitch well in big games against great pitchers. The Rockies also

The Game Changes

Denver's dry air made life difficult on pitchers. But that changed to a certain degree in 2002. That season, the Rockies began storing their baseballs in "The Humidor," a metal box set at 70 degrees and 50 percent humidity. Suddenly, the baseballs were not so dry and they reacted more like they did in other cities. Home runs were still hit at a higher rate at Coors Field than they were at most big-league ballparks. But the sky-high offensive numbers produced at the Rockies' home games in previous years began to drop.

Jeff Francis is shown in 2007. Francis, 17–9 that year, was part of an improved pitching staff that helped the Rockies reach the postseason.

received a boost from youngsters Ubaldo Jimenez, Franklin Morales, and Jason Hirsh. The bullpen, led by All-Star Brian Fuentes, Manuel Corpas, Taylor Buchholz, and veteran Matt Herges, excelled as well.

Everything seemed to work for the Rockies in 2007. For the first time since 1995, they appeared to be on the verge of being a winning team for years to come. They were swept by the mighty Boston Red Sox in the 2007 World Series. But as the Rockies began the 2008 season, confidence was sky high.

The magic of 2007 ran out quickly in 2008, though. The Rockies started slowly and

BORN LEADER

Troy Tulowitzki, known as "Tulo" by Rockies fans, became a leader for Colorado in 2007 despite being a rookie. His will to win and his desire to play the game hard every day have made him a fan favorite. He helped turn the Rockies around.

"We turned a corner as a franchise [in 2007], and the biggest reason for that was Troy," Rockies general manager Dan O'Dowd said. "It's the single-minded focus he brought, that winning comes above everything else. He's one of those very rare players who makes players around him better."

After Tulowitzki finished second in the NL Rookie of the Year voting in 2007 (.291 average, 24 homers, 99 RBIs), he struggled in 2008 while battling injuries. He batted just .263 with eight homers and 46 RBIs in 101 games. He came back strong in 2009. He hit .297 with 32 homers and 92 RBIs and finished fifth in the NL MVP balloting.

never recovered. They finished 74–88 and in third place in the NL West. Everything that worked in 2007 did not work in 2008. Tulowitzki was hurt for much of the year and struggled when he was healthy. Helton, for the first time in his career, was benched by an injury. He missed nearly half the season with a bad back. Francis, after winning 17 games in 2007, went just 4–10 in 2008 while battling a shoulder injury. The same injury kept Francis out for the entire 2009 season as well.

Less than 15 months after the thrill of the World Series, the Rockies were a much different team. The 2008 season brought them back down to earth. After that season, the Rockies made two difficult decisions. They knew that they could not afford Fuentes, their star closer. They let him

Matt Holliday follows through on a swing in 2008. Colorado, looking to save money, traded the star outfielder to Oakland after the season.

go. They also knew they could not afford to keep their best player, Holliday. They traded him to the Oakland Athletics. Matsui and Taveras were also gone by the time the 2009 season rolled around.

Expectations for 2009 were low. Two months into the season, the Rockies went through another major change. With the team sitting at 18–28 in late May, manager Clint Hurdle was fired. Jim Tracy, Colorado's bench coach, took over as the team's manager that day.

The Rockies' players knew that they had to do better. "We need to play the game the right way," Tulowitzki said. "If we do that, winning will take care of itself."

Ubaldo Jimenez prepares to fire a pitch in 2009. Jimenez had a breakout year with 15 wins and helped Colorado make the playoffs. In 2010, he played even better, finishing 19–8 with a 2.88 ERA.

After Hurdle was fired and Tracy took over, the Rockies went 74–42. They finished with a 92–70 record. This was good enough for second place in the NL West and the NL's wild-card spot in the playoffs. It was Colorado's second such postseason berth in three years.

Tulowitzki had an even better year in 2009 than he did in 2007. Helton was healthy again and back to hitting the ball well. The main reason the Rockies made the playoffs in 2009, however, was their pitching. Veteran Jorge De La Rosa led Colorado with 16 wins.

Jimenez, an emerging ace, and veteran Jason Marquis each won 15 games.

Colorado lost three games to one to Philadelphia in the NLDS. Still, by reaching the playoffs twice in three years, the Rockies had achieved a new level of success.

When the Rockies arrived in 1993, they captured the hearts of baseball fans throughout Colorado and the Rocky Mountain region. Fans in the area had been hungry for big-league baseball for years.

As the Rockies finished the 2010 season 83–79, they had captured the hearts of fans for a new reason—they were winners. Stars such as Andres Galarraga, Dante Bichette, Larry Walker, and Matt Holliday had since moved on. But Colorado's future looked brighter than ever. A new core group of young stars—including Tulowitzki,

Jimenez, third baseman Ian Stewart, and outfielder Carlos Gonzalez—had emerged. These players gave the Rockies and their fans reasons for hope in the coming years.

The Holliday Trade

Matt Holliday nearly won the NL MVP Award in 2007. The left fielder finished second in the voting to Philadelphia Phillies shortstop Jimmy Rollins. Holliday led the NL in batting average (.340), RBIs (137), and hits (216) and had 36 home runs. Holliday had a breakout season in 2006 and was an offensive star for Colorado from 2006 to 2008. But because he was so successful, he became an expensive player. As a result, on November, 10, 2008, the Rockies traded him to the Oakland Athletics for pitchers Huston Street and Greg Smith and outfielder Carlos Gonzalez. The trade actually worked out for the Rockies, however. Street excelled as the team's closer in 2009, and Gonzalez, by 2010, was a young star.

1991	On July 5, MLB's 26 team owners vote unanimously to award expansion teams to Denver, Colorado, and South Florida. Those teams would become the Colorado Rockies and the Florida Marlins.
1992	The team starts to take shape when Don Baylor is hired as the Rockies' first manager, first baseman Andres Galarraga signs a free-agent contract, and 36 players are acquired during the expansion draft.
1993	On April 5, the Rockies play their first-ever regular-season game. Colorado loses 3–0 to the host New York Mets at Shea Stadium. David Nied, the Rockies' first pick in the expansion draft, is Colorado's starting pitcher.
1995	Brand-new Coors Field opens in Denver. Playing in their new park, the Rockies reach the playoffs as the NL wild card. They lose to the Atlanta Braves in the NLDS in the first round of the postseason. Baylor is named the NL Manager of the Year.
1997	Right fielder Larry Walker becomes the first Rockie to win the NL MVP Award.
1998	After five seasons, the popular Galarraga leaves Colorado and signs with Atlanta. The Rockies replace him at first base with Todd Helton, who becomes the face of the franchise.
1999	On September 20, Dan O'Dowd is hired as Colorado's general manager. O'Dowd, who had worked in the front offices of the Baltimore Orioles and the Cleveland Indians, eventually helps build the Rockies into a winning franchise.

2005	On June 7, with the seventh pick in MLB's amateur draft, the Rockies select Troy Tulowitzki, a shortstop from Long Beach State. He would make his big-league debut late in the 2006 season and go on to become a star and leader.
2007	The Rockies end the regular season on a remarkable hot streak, going 14–1 in their final 15 games to reach the postseason for the second time. Then, they sweep the Philadelphia Phillies in the NLDS, three games to none, and the Arizona Diamondbacks in the NLCS, four games to none. The Boston Red Sox, however, sweep Colorado four games to none in the World Series.
2007	Matt Holliday finishes as runner-up for the NL MVP Award. Tulowitzki places second in the NL Rookie of the Year voting. Clint Hurdle is third in the NL Manager of the Year race.
2009	On May 29, with the Rockies struggling, Hurdle is fired as manager after nearly eight seasons on the job. He is replaced by bench coach Jim Tracy.
2009	Tracy guides Colorado to a 74–42 record after taking over and is named NL Manager of the Year. With that surge, the Rockies make the playoffs for the second time in three seasons as the NL's wild card. Philadelphia defeats Colorado three games to one in the NLDS.
2010	Ubaldo Jimenez pitches the first no-hitter in Rockies history, leading Colorado to a 4–0 road win over Atlanta on April 17. Jimenez strikes out seven and walks six. The no-hitter is part of a breakout year for Jimenez, who goes 15–1 in the season's first half and is the NL's starting pitcher in the All-Star Game on July 13 in Anaheim, California. Jimenez pitches two scoreless innings in the NL's 3–1 victory over the AL.

QUICK STATS

FRANCHISE HISTORY
1993–

WORLD SERIES
2007

NL CHAMPIONSHIP SERIES
2007

DIVISION CHAMPIONSHIPS
None

WILD-CARD BERTHS
(1995–)

1995, 2007, 2009

KEY PLAYERS
(position[s]; seasons with team)

Dante Bichette (OF; 1993–99)
Vinny Castilla (3B; 1993–99,
    2004, 2006)
Aaron Cook (SP; 2002–)
Brian Fuentes (RP; 2002–08)
Andres Galarraga (1B; 1993–97)
Brad Hawpe (OF; 2004–10)
Todd Helton (1B; 1997–)
Matt Holliday (LF; 2004–08)
Jason Jennings (SP; 2001–06)
Ubaldo Jimenez (SP; 2006–)
Troy Tulowitzki (SS; 2006–)
Eric Young (2B/OF; 1993–97)

KEY MANAGERS

Don Baylor (1993–98):
    440–469; 1–3 (postseason)
Clint Hurdle (2002–09):
    534–625; 7–4 (postseason)
Jim Tracy (2009–):
    157–121; 1–3 (postseason)

HOME PARKS

Mile High Stadium (1993–94)
Coors Field (1995–)

* All statistics through 2010 season

QUOTES AND ANECDOTES

At Coors Field, almost all of the seats are green. There is one row, however, that is colored purple. That row is marked because it is exactly one mile (1.6 km) above sea level.

Several Rockies players might have never played for the team had they chosen different paths. Matt Holliday was a highly recruited high school quarterback and nearly went to Oklahoma State University to play football for the Cowboys. Todd Helton did play quarterback in college, as a backup to Peyton Manning at the University of Tennessee. Another Rockie, Seth Smith, was a backup to quarterback Eli Manning at the University of Mississippi.

"[Before that streak], we all knew we could be a real good team and were better than our record was at the time. But I'm not sure anybody would have predicted a streak like that."
—Left fielder Matt Holliday, on the Rockies' 21–1 record at the end of the 2007 regular season and through the first two rounds of that year's postseason

John Vander Wal never was a starter during his five years with the Rockies, from 1994 to 1998, but he was a valuable player. He was one of the top pinch-hitters in baseball. In 1995, Vander Wal set a major league record with 28 pinch-hits.

The Rockies have a mascot, Dinger, who is a big purple dinosaur. Why a dinosaur? When construction began on Coors Field in 1992, workers dug up a lot of dinosaur bones. Dinger is a tribute to the discovery of those bones. Dinger is on hand for all Rockies home games and is often seen at local events.

GLOSSARY

berth

A place, spot, or position, such as in the baseball playoffs.

cherish

To care for tenderly.

contract

A binding agreement about, for example, years of commitment by a baseball player in exchange for a given salary.

draft

A system used by professional sports leagues to select new players in order to spread incoming talent among all teams.

expansion

In sports, the addition of a franchise or franchises to a league.

franchise

An entire sports organization, including the players, coaches, and staff.

momentum

A continued strong performance based on recent success.

postseason

The games in which the best teams play after the regular-season schedule has been completed.

regard

To show respect or concern for.

rookie

A first-year player in the major leagues.

successor

Someone who follows another person in a particular position.

unanimously

In complete agreement.

zephyr

A gentle or mild breeze. The Denver Zephyrs baseball team was named after the Denver Zephyr passenger train.

FOR MORE INFORMATION

Further Reading

Dater, Adrian. *100 Things Rockies Fans Should Know & Do Before They Die.* Chicago: Triumph Books, 2009.

DeMarco, Tony. *Tales from the Colorado Rockies.* Champaign, IL: Sports Publishing LLC, 2008.

The Denver Post. *A Magical Season: Colorado's Incredible 2007 Championship Season.* Chicago: Triumph Books, 2007.

Web Links

To learn more about the Colorado Rockies, visit ABDO Publishing Company online at **www.abdopublishing.com**. Web sites about the Rockies are featured on our Book Links page. These links are routinely monitored and updated to provide the most current information available.

Places to Visit

Colorado Sports Hall of Fame
INVESCO Field at Mile High
1701 Bryant Street, Suite 500
Denver, CO 80204
720-258-3888
www.coloradosports.org
This hall of fame and museum honors individuals for their athletic accomplishments and leadership in Colorado. Former Rockies first baseman Andres Galarraga is among those who have been inducted.

Coors Field
2001 Blake Street
Denver, CO 80205
303-292-0200
http://mlb.mlb.com/col/ballpark/index.jsp
This has been the Rockies' home field since 1995. The team plays 81 regular-season games here each year.

National Baseball Hall of Fame and Museum
25 Main Street
Cooperstown, NY 13326
888-HALL-OF-FAME
www.baseballhall.org
This hall of fame and museum highlights the greatest players and moments in the history of baseball.

INDEX

About the Author

Brian Howell is a freelance writer based in Denver, Colorado. He has been a sports journalist for more than 17 years. He has covered the Denver Broncos for the past three years for the *Longmont Times-Call* and covered the Colorado Rockies during the 2007 and 2008 seasons. He has earned several writing awards during his career. He lives with his wife and four children.